Pat Ha

Crazy Canadian Trivia

Cover illustration by Bill Dickson

Interior illustrations by Dimitri Kostic

Scholastic Canada Ltd.

Toronto New York London Auckland Sydney
Mexico City New Delhi Hong Kong Buenos Aires

Scholastic Canada Ltd.
604 King Street West, Toronto, Ontario M5V 1E1, Canada

Scholastic Inc.
557 Broadway, New York, NY 10012, USA

Scholastic Australia Pty Limited
PO Box 579, Gosford, NSW 2250, Australia

Scholastic New Zealand Limited
Private Bag 94407, Greenmount, Auckland, New Zealand

Scholastic Children's Books
Euston House, 24 Eversholt Street, London NW1 1DB, UK

*To Sandy, for making me sort through
the piles of clippings, files, books and magazines
in my trivia-cluttered basement in order to do this book.
It was definitely time to do some major tidying.*

The following trademarked names have been used in this book:
Balderdash, Band-Aid, Bubblicious, Crispy Crunch, DOUBLEMINT, JUICY FRUIT,
Mind Trap, Nike, Pictionary, A Question of Scruples, Pogo, Scrabble, Ski-doo,
Tickle Me Elmo, Tilley Hat, Trivial Pursuit, Zamboni.

Library and Archives Canada Cataloguing in Publication

Hancock, Pat
Crazy Canadian trivia / Pat Hancock ; cover art by Bill Dickson ; interior art by Dimitri Kostic.

ISBN 978-0-545-98040-1

1. Canada–Miscellanea–Juvenile literature. I. Dickson, Bill II. Kostic, Dimitri III. Title.

FC58.H28 2009   j971.002   C2009-901149-2

ISBN 10 0-545-98040-2

Introduction

Wild, wacky, wonderful, pretty impressive and absolutely amazing too . . . That would have been a much more descriptive title for this book, but I guess it's a bit long. Okay, the experts were right — it's way too long. It probably wouldn't even fit on a cover.

So, *Crazy Canadian Trivia* it is. But the people you'll meet here, and the things they've done, aren't crazy. I just thought they were all really neat and interesting. That's why I pulled them out of my trivia collection and included them here, along with a bunch of other facts tucked in just for the fun of it.

I may be going a little crazy, though. After this trivia pursuit, my head is so full that I can barely remember where I put my toothbrush. I even forget what else I was going to tell you here. Maybe it'll come to me while you're reading . . .

Pat Hancock

The Strongest Man
in the World

Louis Cyr was born on October 10, 1863, in a little town near Montreal, Saint-Cyprien-de-Napierville. He was a big baby — around 8 kilograms at birth — and he grew up to be a big, powerful, 135-kilogram man. His 61-centimetre biceps were the size of some women's waists, and his 91-centimetre thighs were bigger than the waists of many men.

After he won competitions to determine the strongest man in the United States, and then in Canada, Cyr's fame as the Canadian Hercules began to spread. In his twenties and early thirties he won every strongman and weightlifting competition in Canada and the United States. When he went to London, England, in 1892 and lifted 1652 kilograms on his back and 250 kilograms with one finger, everyone agreed that he was indeed the strongest man in the world.

Funny Money

For nearly 80 years, starting in 1685, playing cards were as good as gold in Canada. During that time, they were used like money in New France, France's colony in North America back then.

When real money was in short supply, the governor would have some playing cards cut into quarters, and assign each part a value equal to a certain number of French coins. To make them official, the cards were marked with the treasurer's wax seal, and signed by the governor and his intendant or business manager.

When supply ships finally arrived from France with money from the king or from the sale of furs sent back to Europe the year before, people could cash in their card money for the real thing.

The Buck Stopped Here

And speaking of money, it was a chemistry professor working at Montreal's McGill University who came up with the ink the United States chose to print their money with, from 1862 onward. Professor Thomas Sterry Hunt's special green ink couldn't be reproduced by photography, making it almost impossible for forgers to churn out fake "greenbacks," the nickname given to American bills.

Ice Cream, Anyone?

July 24, 1988, wasn't just another workday for the folks at Palm Dairy in Edmonton, Alberta. Under the watchful eye of supervisor Mike Rogiani they shovelled and shaped 20 313 kilograms of ice cream into a huge mound. Then they ladled on 4404 kilos of syrup, followed by 244 kilos of toppings. *Voilà* — the world's biggest sundae!

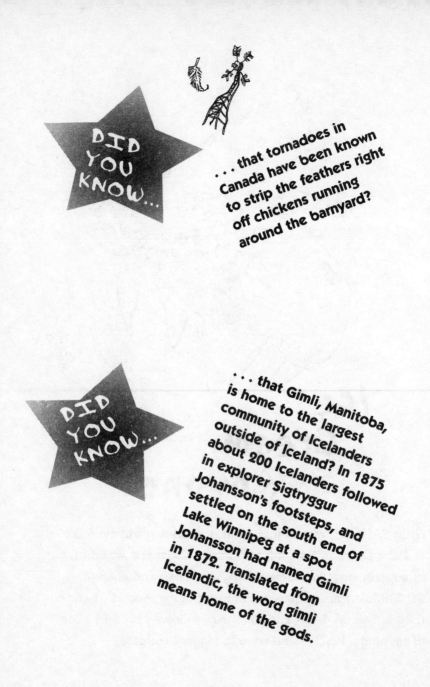

DID YOU KNOW... ... that tornadoes in Canada have been known to strip the feathers right off chickens running around the barnyard?

DID YOU KNOW... ... that Gimli, Manitoba, is home to the largest community of Icelanders outside of Iceland? In 1875 about 200 Icelanders followed in explorer Sigtryggur Johansson's footsteps, and settled on the south end of Lake Winnipeg at a spot Johansson had named Gimli in 1872. Translated from Icelandic, the word gimli means home of the gods.

Highest High Tide

The Bay of Fundy, between New Brunswick and southwest Nova Scotia, has the largest tides in the world. High tide at the head of the bay can reach heights of up to 16 metres! The surging ebb and flow of the ocean in this part of the world is also what causes an impressive natural phenomenon — the reversing falls on the Saint John River, near Saint John, New Brunswick. When the tide is going out, water flows over a rock shelf near the river's mouth and out into the sea. But as the tide comes in, the level of the river rises to the point where water starts spilling over the shelf back into the river, in effect changing the direction of the waterfall.

The Greatest Athletes in Their Field

Two members of the Canadian Sports Hall of Fame aren't people, but horses. Northern Dancer, the greatest Canadian racehorse ever, was named to the Hall in 1965. He sired over 1000 foals. Some people believe that his lineage will result in more champions than any horse that ever lived.

World champion show jumper Big Ben and his human partner Ian Millar both became Hall of Famers in 1996.

© Shawn Hamilton/CLiX

Two boats are also members of the Hall of Fame — the *Bluenose* and *Miss Supertest III*. The *Bluenose*, the elegant schooner pictured on the Canadian dime and on the stamp below, was one of the greatest sailing ships ever built. From 1921 to 1938 she was also the fastest, winning every sailing race she entered. She and her winning captain, Angus Walters, were made members of the Hall of Fame in 1955.

Miss Supertest III was a world champion speedboat. She and her pilot, Robert Hayward, ruled the world hydroplane racing circuit from 1959 to 1961, and entered the Hall in 1960.

CANADA 37

Angus Walters Captain/Capitaine Bluenose

© Canada Post Corporation, 1988. Reproduced by permission.

A Secret Life

When Leslie McFarlane died in 1977, one newspaper article remembered him as Canada's best-selling author ever. That came as a surprise to a lot of people. McFarlane had been a well respected and successful writer, playwright, scriptwriter and film director — but best-selling novelist hadn't been his claim to fame. That's because until he wrote his autobiography in 1976, no one knew that he had written nearly two dozen of the most popular American adventure stories for boys.

In his autobiography, McFarlane revealed that he was Franklin W. Dixon, the author of the *HARDY BOYS* series. He wrote the series for Edward L. Stratemeyer, a hugely successful American publisher, himself a series writer for younger readers. Stratemeyer paid McFarlane a small fee for each story, rather than giving him a percentage from each book sold, and made him promise not to tell anyone that he was Franklin W. Dixon. That's why no one knew that McFarlane's books had sold over 12 million copies — not even his own children! He had kept his secret for nearly 50 years.

No Free Lunch

A few wilderness hikers like to use pack animals — horses, donkeys, mules or even llamas — to carry their gear. But whichever animals they use, they need to make sure to pack food for them as well as for themselves, if they're trekking through one of Canada's national parks. Without food, the animals might start nibbling on the park's grass. And that's a no-no. Hikers will be fined unless they can produce a special permit that allows the animals to graze.

Colour-Coded Critters

If you're in Toronto or Montreal, check out the squirrels that live there. Most of the squirrels in Montreal are grey, whereas 80 percent of Toronto's are black. And in Exeter, Ontario, these frisky cousins of the rat are all white. Go figure.

DID YOU KNOW...

... that Ontario is the worst place in the world for hay fever sufferers? Apparently, ragweed plants love the growing conditions in parts of the province. Worse still, the plant's pollen — the part that causes the allergic reactions — can really get around, travelling up to 300 kilometres through the air. Ahhhhh-choo!

What's That, Eh?

Canadians have definitely had a long love affair with hockey, so it shouldn't surprise anyone to learn that the word deke originated in Canada. A shortened version of decoy, the word refers to a false move or faked shot intended to fool an opponent. *The Complete Oxford English Dictionary* lists deke's first recorded appearance in print in a hockey news item in the *Kingston Whig Standard* newspaper in 1961.

Caddy for Hire

For five years after it opened in 1997 the nine-hole River Valley Golf and Country Club near Stratford, Ontario, had some super-strong caddies. They were llamas, South American members of the camel family that look a lot like dromedaries, but without a hump.

The llamas were a big hit with golfers. They could carry two sets of golf clubs without working up a sweat. But they wouldn't put up with being overloaded. Pile too much on them and they'd just sit down and refuse to budge.

13

MOVING DAY

While most other Canadians are enjoying the July 1 Canada Day holiday, nearly 200 000 renters in Montreal are caught up in moving-day madness. Most apartment leases expire on June 30, leaving tenants scrambling to shift their furniture and belongings from one place to the next all at the same time.

Trucks and moving vans have to be booked months in advance, often at hourly rates three to four times higher than usual. And even if you're lucky enough to rent one of those vehicles, you still have to figure out ways to get your furniture down the stairs while two or three other tenants are trying to get theirs up. People pile their stuff on lawns and sidewalks, waiting for old tenants to move out. Rain can turn the entire process into an even bigger nightmare than it already is.

Seas of Red and Blue

The Lower Fraser River Valley of British Columbia is the cranberry capital of Canada. The areas around Richmond, Fort Langley and Pitt Meadows produce 80 percent of the cranberries grown in Canada, and B.C. berries regularly pass the bounce test with flying colours. Bounce test?

Processing plants use what are called bounceboard separators to weed out inferior berries. Apparently, fresh, firm crimson berries bounce like mini ping-pong balls, but rotten or withered berries just sit there when the bounceboard goes into action.

On the other side of the country, the berry scene changes colour. Nova Scotia is Canada's top blueberry producer, and Oxford, Nova Scotia, is the nation's blueberry capital.

Canadians love their telephones. They spend more time talking on the phone than people in any other country in the world.

. . . that there are no skunks in Newfoundland? And Alberta does an excellent job of keeping out rats. Although a few have been known to slip in uninvited, officially there are no rats in the province.

SASKATCHEWAN

. . . that the St. John's Regatta — a series of boat races held annually in Newfoundland — is the longest-running sporting event in North America? The regatta was first held in 1818.

A Deep-Sea Giant

The Pacific waters off the coast of British Columbia are home to the world's largest species of octopus, *Octopus dofleini*. This eight-armed monster of the deep can grow up to 9 metres wide and weigh more than 100 kilograms. Tinted a dark red, it can change colour to blend in with its surroundings, and if it loses one of its arms, it can grow it back. Like other octopi, it squirts out dark ink when it's being threatened so that it can make a quick escape under cover of the darkness.

Researchers who have studied these creatures think that they're very smart and can teach each others what they've learned. Thank goodness they haven't learned to slip aboard boats yet and hitch a ride.

What's
That, Eh?

Unless you're a real con artist, you won't have much luck selling a moose pasture to anyone with a brain. A moose pasture is a very Canadian expression describing a piece of worthless land.

Ladies and Gentlemen, Start Your Bathtubs!

Nanaimo, British Columbia, is the second largest city on Vancouver Island. It's separated from the mainland by the Strait of Georgia. On the third Sunday in July each year, thousands of spectators head across that strait to take in one of the wackiest water races in the world — the Nanaimo International Bathtub Race. Originally a 1967 Centennial celebration involving only real old-fashioned bathtubs, the race now attracts some pretty amazing watercraft made out of fibreglass. But no matter what they're made of they still must look like your basic, roll-edged bathtub with a motor on one end. And no souped-up engines are allowed. Members of the Loyal Nanaimo Bathtub Society make sure of that.

Sweet City Square

Nanaimo also lays claim to another international success – the melt-in-your-mouth chocolate treat that bears its name. Rumours abound about where the layered square got its start, or what it was called originally, but there's no doubt about which place has adopted it and given it a permanent home. City officials give visitors a best-ever-recipe rating for Nanaimo Bars, and the city's unofficial mascot is – you guessed it – a walking, talking Nanaimo Bar named Nanaimo Barney.

Apparently, one or two recipes for Nanaimo Bar look-alikes did appear in British and American cookbooks early on, but there's no doubt that another sweet treat is strictly Canadian. Gooey-delicious raisin-filled butter tarts were born in the kitchens of Canadian pioneer families. Mmmmmmm-good for them.

DID YOU KNOW...

... that the only animals in Canada's largest circus, the world-renowned *Cirque du Soleil*, are of the human kind? These fantastic performers don't need elephants and lions to draw people into their big tent. They wow audiences with their own incredible acrobatic feats and choreographic artistry.

DID YOU KNOW...

... that people in British Columbia drove on the left side of the road until January 1, 1922? And did you know that it was J. D. Millar, an engineer working for the Ontario Department of Highways, who came up with the brilliant idea of painting broken lines on roads to both mark the middle and to indicate that it was safe to pass if you couldn't see any oncoming traffic? Millar got this brainwave back in 1930.

Storm of the Century

© Department of National Defence/
Corporal Tom Sullivan

A six-day ice storm mercilessly battered eastern Ontario, Quebec and the Maritimes from January 4-10 in 1998. Weighed down under layers of ice as thick as 8 centimetres, millions of trees splintered like toothpicks and thousands of kilometres of power lines snapped like over-stretched guitar strings. The storm did at least $500 million damage and left 1 673 000 customers without electricity, nearly 1 400 000 of those in Quebec alone.

Sap It Up

Many of the trees damaged during the 1998 Quebec ice storm were maples, putting a dint in the country's annual maple syrup production. Quebec produces 90 percent of this traditionally Canadian syrup. It takes 40 litres of sap to boil up 1 litre of the genuine article. Fake maple syrup is just plain glucose with artificial flavouring. Quebeckers have a name for such a pitiful pretender. They call it *sirop de poteau* — telephone pole or dead-tree syrup.

In June, 1988, folks in Lefaivre, west of Hawkesbury, Ontario, needed all the syrup they could get to serve up a record-breaking pancake. Local Lions Club members mixed, poured, flipped and cooked a 9.14-metre-wide flapjack that weighed 909 kilograms.

Mortal Danger

In early April, 1996, keepers of Wiarton Willie announced that the famed weather-predicting gopher from Wiarton, Ontario, was being kept in protective custody. Town officials were responding to death threats made by angry callers who felt Willie had let them down. He had promised everyone an early spring, but winter was still hanging around.

Three years later, a long line of mourners paid their last respects to the shadow-fearing critter. News of Wiarton Willie's death from natural causes brought messages of condolence from around the world. But sympathy turned to anger once again when people who had filed past the tiny wooden casket learned that the stiff little body in the coffin was a pretender to the weather-predicting throne.

When keepers had gone to check on Willie in his den and make sure he was ready to make an appearance on February 2, Groundhog Day, they were shocked to find that he had passed away sometime during the winter . . . and what was left of him wasn't a pretty sight. So they tucked a stuffed, glass-eyed substitute into the coffin and displayed it to the thousands of visitors attending the Wiarton Willie Winter Festival. Saddened mourners said they felt betrayed. *Realllly?*

Smelling a Rat

Some Halifax residents got a bit of a scare on February 2, 2000, during radio station CFRQ's coverage of a local version of Wiarton Willie's weather-predicting efforts. Claiming that the city wouldn't spend money for a real groundhog, the station reported that a sewer rat — Waterfront Willie — had been recruited instead.

But when the time came for the waterfront rat to make his debut, a news announcer reporting live by cellphone said Willie wouldn't come out and he was going to poke him with a stick. Then the horrified-sounding reporter started describing in gory detail how the enraged Willie was tearing into the limbs of city officials on hand for the ceremonies. Suddenly the cellphone went dead . . . and the station's switchboard lit up. Worried listeners wanted to know what had happened to the announcer. That's when the real announcers decided to come clean. There was no Waterfront Willie, and the report of carnage was a fake. The whole thing had just been a hoax intended to spice up a bland February morning.

More Pickles, Please

No Canadians have made the record books for crunching down a gross number of dill pickles, but two Canadian brothers did become household names when they started producing a favourite of dill-pickle lovers in Canada and the United States. Daniel and Irving Strub emigrated from Russia to Hamilton, Ontario, with their parents in 1921. They loved their mother's homemade pickles, and figured others would too. When they were old enough, they started their own pickle-pickling company, using their mom's recipe. Dill-pickle connoisseurs loved the plump, crunchy, brine-pickled cucumbers, and they still do. The Strub plant, which moved to Brantford, Ontario, in 1991, now produces more than 500 barrels of pickles a day.

Pass the Pickles

Some people will do almost anything to set a new world record. In 1978, Patrick Donahue made a grab for his fifteen minutes of fame in Victoria, B.C. That's where he wolfed down 91 pickled onions in just 1 minute and 8 seconds. The price of glory? Onion burps and a bloated belly.

Thank goodness no official was around to enforce a law that's supposedly still included in Canada's criminal code. Apparently, it's illegal to offend a public place with a bad smell.

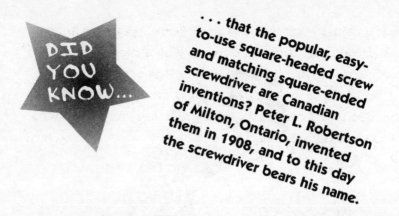

Long, Longer, Longest

If you're into making long trips, Canada is definitely the place to be. The ultimate challenge would be to hike along or sail in and out of every bay and inlet along Canada's coastline, the longest in the world. As Statistics Canada points out, if it were stretched out into a straight line, it would reach two-thirds of the way to the moon.

A somewhat saner trip would be a drive across the country on the world's longest national highway, the Trans-Canada Highway. It's 7821 kilometres long. If you prefer a shorter journey that's still pretty impressive, you can wend your way from Toronto to Rainy River, Ontario, on the longest street in the world. Yonge Street, Toronto's main thoroughfare, reaches all the way to the Ontario-Minnesota border, a distance of more than 1900 kilometres.

And if you just want to spend a few hours breathing in brisk winter air, you can head to Ottawa and glide along the world's longest skating rink, a 7.8-kilometre section of the Rideau Canal. Daily traffic and weather reports even include updated information on ice conditions for those hardy commuters who skate to work each morning.

Bridging the Gap

Confederation Bridge links New Brunswick to Prince Edward Island. There's no question about it — at 12.9 kilometres, this engineering wonder is the longest bridge in the world built over water that's sometimes ice-covered. But another question remains: is an island still an island if you can get there by car? That's under debate in P.E.I., the province that's been dubbed the biggest farm in Canada. (By the way, the dirt there really is red.)

Kissing Bridge

The 339-metre-long wooden bridge at Hartland, New Brunswick, is one of Canada's most popular tourist attractions. It's the longest covered bridge in the world. Some people think that the bridge was covered over to keep out the snow, but that's not true. Locals actually used to haul snow *onto* the bridge so that horse-drawn sleighs could cross it easily in the winter. But covers on bridges like this one did keep them drier and stop the wooden planks from rotting too quickly. They also kept spying neighbours from watching courting couples as they drove across the bridge in carriages or sleighs. That's why they were often called kissing bridges.

How Low Can You Go?

Probably not as low as 15-year-old Marlene Raymond did when she limboed under a flaming bar at the Port of Spain Pavilion during Toronto's Caravan Festival in 1973. On June 24 that year she set a new world record for limbo dancing when she cleared a burning bar that was just 16.5 centimetres off the ground!

Big Apples

Canada's own McIntosh apple is a really big hit around the world. It's so well recognized as something wonderfully delicious that it's even used as the logo for a top-brand computer. Over half of the 17 million or so bushels of apples grown in Canada every year are crisp, juicy Macs, and every one of them can be traced back to one tree that farmer John McIntosh found growing on his St. Lawrence River Valley farm in 1811.

No one knows for certain how that apple tree came to be growing in the woods McIntosh was clearing at his new homestead. But we do know that if his son, Allan, hadn't figured out how to graft cuttings from it onto other apple trees, there wouldn't be any McIntosh apples around today.

Another Canadian big apple catches the eye of every traveller on Ontario's Highway 401 near Colborne, Ontario. You can't miss it. It's bright red — naturally — and it's 10.7 metres tall and 11.6 metres wide. This 42-tonne structure doubles as a restaurant and tourist information site in a region of the country very proud of the apples grown there. Ontario produces about 400 million Macs a year.

Top Dog On October 5, 1990, children's author Jean Little received an honourary doctorate from Ontario's University of Guelph, in her own home town.

Little was named a "doctor of letters, *honoris causa*." But she wasn't the only one in the spotlight at that graduation ceremony. University president Brian Segal presented Little's seeing-eye dog, Zephyr, with his own special degree: "doctor of litters, *honoris canine*." Little accepted the honour on Zephyr's behalf. Having guided his owner safely to the stage, the Labrador retriever was settled down beside her, snoozing.

The Labrador retriever is a Canadian breed of dog. Both black and golden Labs often graduate with top honours from schools that train dogs to guide the blind. One of the breed also achieved hero status on December 11, 1919.

On that fateful day, the *S.S. Ethie*, battered by hurricane-force winds, ran aground off the west coast of Newfoundland, north of the Bay of Islands. One sailor shot a rope from the boat to the shore, but it fell short among some offshore rocks. Local residents couldn't reach it, but one of their dogs did. The brave animal fought its way through the huge icy waves breaking over the rocks, bit onto the end of the line, and swam with it back to shore. With the rope secured, all 60 passengers and 32 crew members aboard the *Ethie* were eventually rescued.

An Owner's Manual for a Hat?

That's right. There is a hat that actually comes with a four-page owner's manual, and it's very, very Canadian. The manual for the made-in-Canada Tilley Hat tells you how to wear it, how to clean it, and — in case you can't figure it out on your own — how to tell the front from the back. It even tells you how to rescue the hat if it falls overboard when you're sailing.

The creation of Torontonian Alex Tilley in 1980, this hat has become the darling of travellers around the world. Canadian peacekeepers wear it proudly abroad, and it's Everest-climber Sir Edmund Hillary's favourite headgear. One reason for the Tilley hat's popularity is that it's nearly indestructible. And if it does wear out, you can get a replacement for free. (That's not likely to happen, though. One Tilley owner claims that an elephant ate his hat, and when the hat "re-emerged" a day later, a good wash was all it needed. Good thing — the elephant ate the hat not just once, but three times!)

Another Top Hat

Another made-in-Canada hat that took the world by storm was the jaunty red Roots creation Canadian athletes wore at the 1998 Winter Olympics in Nagano, Japan. It was such a hot item that the athletes had a hard time keeping it on their heads. The "poor boy" caps quickly became a hit with celebrities looking to make a fashion statement, too. Without an owner's manual to guide them, some people wore it backwards, but that didn't matter. It looked great either way.

What's That, Eh?

Be careful about asking for your bunny hug in front of English-speaking visitors from another country. Not knowing what that is, they might crush you in a "bear hug," instead of handing you your warm sweatshirt with an attached hood.

On Your Mark . . .
Get Set . . .
Kiss!

On the night before Valentine's Day in 1999, 1543 pairs of lovebirds gathered at the Sports and Entertainment Centre in Sarnia, Ontario. But they weren't there for a romantic dinner or cheek-to-cheek dancing. They were there to chalk up a lip-locking new world record for the most couples to kiss each other at the same time in the same place. What did love have to do with it? Well, maybe not all that much, but it was fun while it lasted.

Channel Watching

The Viewer Chip, or V-chip, that parents can use to block violent or otherwise offensive television shows from coming into their homes is a Canadian invention. It's the work of Tim Collins, a professor at the Technical University of British Columbia in Surrey, B.C.

These Shoes Aren't Meant for Walking

The world's biggest and best collection of shoes, boots, sandals and everything else related to footwear is housed in the Bata Shoe Museum in Toronto. The museum's 10 000-piece collection covers 4500 years of footwear history. It's also home to such cool items as Elvis Presley's blue-and-white patent leather loafers, prima ballerina Karen Kain's pointe shoes, Elton John's silver platform boots, Louis Riel's snowshoes, Queen Victoria's satin flats and the Nike trainers David Bowie wore on his Serious Moonlight tour.

What's That, Eh?

Want to nosh on a Pogo? Pogo is the brand name for a Canadian-made junk food treat. Popular first in Quebec, it's now even showing up in the frozen food section of the supermarket. Haven't had one yet? Well, it's a hot dog dipped in cornmeal batter that's then deep-fried or baked, and served on a stick.

The Ice Man Rules

Jimmy "The Ice Man" MacNeil rode his Zamboni with pride. Fans at the Brantford, Ontario, Civic Centre cheered him on whenever he drove his big ice scraper out between periods of Junior B hockey games. But he got a lot more than local recognition when an e-mail contest to choose the best Zamboni driver in North America caught fire during the summer and fall of 1999. When Brantford fans learned of the contest, they nominated their very own Ice Man, and then began to spread the word. MacNeil was definitely the underdog, going up against Zamboni drivers from some of the National Hockey League's top arenas. But Canadians — some of the world's heaviest users of the Internet — rallied around him, and their votes started flooding in. To the amazement of contest organizers, MacNeil won the contest. He was the new North American Zamboni champion!

NHL officials hadn't expected this result. The winner was slated to clean the ice during the All-Star game on February 6, 2000, at the Toronto Maple Leaf's new home, the Air Canada Centre. But the regular Air Canada Centre Zamboni drivers weren't about to let the supposedly inexperienced MacNeil loose on their ice. Still, MacNeil wasn't bitter. He did get to drive a ceremonial victory lap around the arena.

Ketchup
or
Vinegar?

Canada is the world's largest producer of frozen french fries. Maritime food giant McCain Foods Ltd. can take credit for this Canadian claim to fame.

And just for the record, instant mashed potatoes are a Canadian invention. They were first cooked up by Edward Asselbergs, a research scientist with Canada's Department of Agriculture. He patented his flaky recipe in 1961.

On the west coast, Pemberton, British Columbia, can claim its share of spud glory. Although a sign at the outskirts of town warns, "The planting of potatoes is prohibited," Pemberton is home to nearly 170 fields of potatoes. But these aren't just any old potatoes. Pemberton spuds are started in sterile labs and planted in carefully tended fields to make sure that they are free of diseases that commonly attack potato plants. That's why they are in such demand as seed potatoes with many North American growers. It's also why any unauthorized growing of potatoes is strictly forbidden.

Summer Never Came

People in Canada and the northern United States liked to keep a copy of *The Old Farmer's Almanac* handy. Published annually, this small book contains all sorts of interesting news, household hints and farming advice. It also offers weather predictions for the entire next year. In 1815, one of the typesetters preparing the 1816 almanac for printing decided to have a little fun. He slipped in a fake prediction of snow, hail and rain for July 13, 1816. Imagine everyone's surprise months later when it did exactly that.

And not just on that day. On June 5, bitter Arctic winds had swept through eastern Canada, killing crops in the fields and leaves on the trees, and giving people in Quebec and Montreal a major snowstorm. And if that wasn't enough, the area was hit with a killer frost at the beginning of August, and another major snowfall on August 21.

Not surprisingly, 1816 became known as the "year without a summer." It was also the year when many people who had ended up with one of those altered copies of the almanac became faithful followers of the almanac's year-in-advance weather forecasts.

Just a Kid

In 2000, famed hockey great Henri "The Pocket Rocket" Richard was still younger than all the National Hockey League players who joined the NHL forty years after he did. How? Well, if you're counting birthdays, he just turned 16 in 2000. That's because his birthday is February 29, and that day usually only comes around once every four years. The former Montreal Canadiens star is one of about 21 000 Canadians who are leap-year babies. In non-leap years, most of them choose to celebrate their big day on February 28. They might have had to do that again in 2000 if that number couldn't be divided evenly by 400. Unless a turn-of-the-century year — such as 1800, 1900, 2000 or 2100 — is divisible by 400, leaving no remainder, it isn't a leap year. Then "leapers" have to wait *another* four years for their official big day.

DID YOU KNOW...

· · · that Canada's favourite chocolate bar is Crispy Crunch? How about younger Canucks' favourite bubble gum? Bubblicious tops that list, but adults prefer their gum minty. On average, Canadians chew about 1 kilogram of gum each year.

Hoop Dreams

Next to soccer, basketball is the most popular sport in the world, and all those exciting slam dunks can be traced right back to James Naismith, the Canadian from Almonte, Ontario, who invented the game. Naismith came up with the idea of trying to shoot a soccer ball through a peach basket on December 21, 1891, when he was working as a physical education director at a YMCA in Springfield, Massachusetts. Over the next few weeks, Naismith tidied up his rules for the new indoor sport, and the first proper game was played in January, 1892.

Fifty-four years later, Canadians again made basketball history. On November 1, 1946, the Toronto Huskies hosted the New York Knicks at Toronto's Maple Leaf Gardens. This match was, in effect, the first National Basketball League game ever played. The Huskies were one of the founding members of the Basketball Association of America, which went on to become the NBA. However, the Huskies only lasted a year. They also lost that first game against the Knicks 68–66.

Silent Terror

On March 30, 1848, people living near Niagara Falls woke up to a terrifying sound — the sound of silence. The night before, so much ice had built up in Lake Erie that it had dammed up the water that usually poured into the Niagara River and raced over the Falls. But local residents didn't know this. All they knew was that the never-ending torrent that had become so familiar to them was gone. When they dressed and rushed to the river's edge, they stood in awe. The Falls had stopped falling!

Some people were so worried by this unnatural sight that they rushed off to attend special church services held to calm their fears. A few more daring folks took advantage of this once-in-a-lifetime chance to scramble over the rocks at the bottom of the Falls, or to walk across the mighty river that had been reduced to a trickle.

The next night, changing winds broke up the ice-jam and water started to surge out of the lake and into the river once more. In just a matter of minutes, water from the Falls was falling again. The familiar roar was music to people's ears.

FALLS STOPS FALLING!

Unbelievable!

On July 9, 1960, seven-year-old Roger Woodward and his seventeen-year-old sister, Deanne, went for a Saturday afternoon boat ride with a family friend, Jim Honeycutt. After several minutes putt-putting down the Niagara River, the boat's propeller hit a rock and broke. Without power, the boat was caught in the grip of the river's surging current. Honeycutt started rowing furiously, but the boat capsized in the rushing water, tossing the terrified threesome overboard.

Roger and Deanne were both wearing life jackets, but they were no match for the river. Just a few metres from the Falls, Deanne was grabbed by a quick-thinking bystander, but Roger and Honeycutt were swept over the brink. Incredibly, as Roger tumbled into the swirling whirlpool below, he was spotted by the captain of the *Maid of the Mist*, a boat that regularly takes tourists on the ride of their lives beneath the Falls. Young Roger managed to grab hold of a life preserver thrown from the boat. When he was hauled to safety on board, the first thing he asked for, trembling and gasping, was a drink of water.

Both Roger and his sister recovered completely from their brush with death, but the Falls had claimed one more victim. Honeycutt's body was found four days later.

Out in Left Field?

The year 1999 was a great year for CPRC — Circles Phenomenon Research Canada. It's a group that tracks and studies the sudden mysterious appearances of circular shapes in farmers' fields. In 1999 the group recorded a record number of crop circles in Canada, 20 in all. Saskatchewan, a popular gallery for such geometric field art, topped the list with 10. The circles showed up in prairie wheat fields, blueberry fields and cornfields in six provinces.

Many people think the shapes are the work of pranksters who sneak into the fields at night and trample down the plants. Others say unusual swirling winds cause them. But CPRC members aren't so sure what's going on. Still, they aren't ready to blame aliens either — the usual suspects when easy explanations are hard to come by.

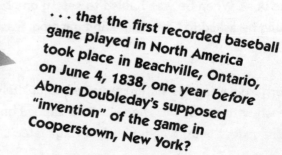

DID YOU KNOW...

... that the first recorded baseball game played in North America took place in Beachville, Ontario, on June 4, 1838, one year before Abner Doubleday's supposed "invention" of the game in Cooperstown, New York?

Guard Duty

Firefighters got more than they bargained for when they answered an alarm in a Montreal apartment building early in February, 2000. When they broke into a smoke-filled flat, they didn't have too much trouble putting out the fire. But they weren't too sure how to handle the big boa constrictor and 1.5-metre-long alligator left to guard the hundreds of marijuana plants growing in the place. The plants' owners were nowhere to be found.

That same month, a Winnipeg teenager was very happy to be found when firefighters arrived at her home. In fact, Rhiannon Bruyère says she might have died of smoke inhalation if it hadn't been for her animal housemate. She woke up in the middle of the night to find her tiny black kitten, Daisy, pawing at her face. Then she smelled the smoke. Thanks to Daisy, Bruyère and two other residents were able to escape to safety.

Want to Be a Millionaire?

Toronto high school students Michael Furdyk and Albert Lau, and Michael Hayman of Australia, met over the Internet because they shared the same hobby — computers. Soon they were giving each other computer tips and helping other Internet users solve problems. Then the three teens decided to start publishing an Internet magazine, *My Desktop*, where they could share their hobby with even more computer users. Obviously, people were hungry for information and advice on running their home computers. *My Desktop* took off, receiving thousands of hits from Web surfers each week.

Lau, Furdyk and Hayman finally got to meet in person in the summer of 1998. By then they had a business plan in place and had turned *My Desktop* into a legally incorporated business. The magazine's popularity continued to soar, and by the spring of 1999 it was receiving more than 5 million hits a month. That's when an American company stepped in and offered the young partners nearly $1.5 million (U.S.) for their hobby-turned-business. It was an offer they couldn't refuse.

... that moose were once used
to haul mail in the Edmonton
area? Caribou also did the job
in Labrador every now and then.

... that in 1997 soccer beat out
hockey as Canada's top sport when
it comes to the number of registered
players in competitive leagues?

Maple Hits a Home Run

For nearly 70 years, batters in major league baseball games could use only bats made from ash trees. But when the new season opened in the spring of 1998, that rule changed. The league officially approved the use of the new Sam Bat, made by Ottawa carpenter Sam Holman. Holman makes his bats out of Canadian maple trees because maple is harder and doesn't dent or break as easily as ash. When the Baseball Hall of Fame in Cooperstown, New York, learned the Sam Bat had been approved, it got one to include in its hall of famous bats that have been swung into baseball history.

Larry Walker's bat was pretty special too. It took him all the way from his hometown of Maple Ridge, B. C., to the big leagues of professional baseball. Only a few Canadians have done that, and he was the first one of them to make it to the top. On November 13, 1997, the 30-year-old outfielder for the Colorado Rockies was named the most valuable player in the National League. Nine years later, Justin Morneau, another Canadian — and another British Columbian — matched Walker's achievement when he was named the American League's MVP for 2006.

REST IN PEACE

When Marie Louise Meilleur died in Corbeil, Ontario, on April 16, 1998, her family mourned her passing, but the world also took notice. In August, 1997, when she celebrated her 117th birthday, Mrs. Meilleur had officially become the oldest living person in the world. Born on August 29, 1880, in rural Quebec, Meilleur moved to Ontario in 1911 after her first husband died, and she married again. Much loved by all who knew her, she was survived by 4 of her children, 85 grandchildren, 80 great-grandchildren, 57 great-great-grandchildren and 4 great-great-great-grandchildren.

Psssst . . .
Wanna Buy a Cup o' Poop?

If you did, then the tiny village of Desmond, Ontario, a few kilometres north of Napanee, was the place to go. Throughout most of the 1990s it claimed to be the manure capital of Ontario, and maybe of the world. For nine years it hosted "Manurefest," a celebration of you-know-what, and there was plenty of it to go around. You name it; they had it — from chickens, rabbits, sheep, pigs, horses and cows. If you were a serious gardener, you could pick up a 20-kilogram sack of the stuff. But if you just wanted to give one of your houseplants a boost, you could buy a "Cup o' Poop," a small bag of it neatly stuffed into a disposable coffee cup.

Better Late Than Never

In 1984, hockey superstar Wayne Gretzky was named to the Order of Canada. But winter's a busy time for someone with a job like Gretzky's, and he was doing his rather well, so he couldn't make it to the ceremonies in Ottawa to receive his medal. His team needed him then, and for the next 13 winters when the Order of Canada ceremonies were held.

But by January, 1998, Gretzky was playing for the New York Rangers, and they just happened to be in the capital to play the Ottawa Senators. Finally the Great One was able to visit Rideau Hall when the Order of Canada ceremonies were taking place. So, on January 28, 1998 — 14 years later — Gretzky proudly received his medal from Governor General Roméo LeBlanc.

The **Great** One Is the **Greatest**

During his career, Gretzky tied or broke an incredible 61 records — some of them his own. Here's just a sampling of his record-breaking accomplishments:
- most regular season career goals (894 in 1487 games)
- most goals, including playoff games (1016)
- most goals in one season (92)
- most regular season career assists (1963)
- most assists, including playoffs (2223)
- most career points, including playoffs (3239)
- most 100-or-more point seasons (15)
- most career playoff goals (122)
- most career playoff assists (260)
- most game-winning playoff goals (24)

In 1999, Gretzky bid farewell to the sport he loved with a passion, and the National Hockey League retired his jersey number, 99, forever.

If You Can't Beat Them, Join Them

Janet and Gerry McKay called their farm at Rimbey, north of Red Deer, Alberta, the Bloomin' Idiot Funny Farm. Like the rest of us, the McKays had to put up with buzzing, blood-hungry mosquitoes during the summer months. But instead of crying in their insect repellent, they finally decided to befriend the enemy. They set up little houses where "mozzies" could breed in peace, and in 1994, they founded SWAMP, the Society for Wild Alberta Mosquito Preservation. Then they started selling lifetime memberships in SWAMP to other "Bloomin' Idiots." Members got tiny playground toys and a miniature outhouse to make mosquitoes feel right at home.

In 1998, the McKays started pushing for a special national Mosquito Appreciation Day — MAD. They figured January 31 would be a great choice for MAD, since on that day you'd have to hold off swatting any of the annoying little pests. The idea didn't catch on.

Researchers in Winnipeg say that Canadian mosquitoes are nastier than most of the other 3000 or so species found throughout the world. You'll get no argument about that from people in Manitoba. Supposedly, it ties with Louisiana as the mosquito capital of North America.

Whether you're a francophone or an anglophone, you know exactly where to go if someone asks you to pick up a loaf of bread at the dépanneur. Dépanneur is what you call a corner store or convenience store in Quebec. Like a dépanneur (road mechanic) who rescues you when your car breaks down, the corner store is there for you when you need something in a hurry or don't want to go all the way to a large supermarket.

Doing the Salt Crawl

If you decided to take a dip in Patience Lake, southeast of Saskatoon, Saskatchewan, you wouldn't have to worry too much about sinking. The water in Patience Lake is ten times saltier than sea water, making it denser and much easier to float in than fresh water. But Patience Lake isn't as unusual as you might think. More than 500 Saskatchewan lakes, ranging in size from 4 to 180 square metres, are salty.

Muscle Power

Pedal power ruled in the spring of 1982 when Brock Allison set off from Vancouver on May 1, on a trip across Canada. On June 26 he arrived in Halifax. It had taken him 56 days and 10.75 hours to ride 5947.7 kilometres — on his unicycle!

Three years later, from August 10–12, 25-year-old David Frank rode his skateboard back and forth and around and around in Toronto. He pushed and rolled 432.77 kilometres in 36 hours, 43 minutes, 42 seconds — earning himself a place in the record books.

And two years after that, in February, 1987, John Sarish showed off his record-breaking muscle power in London, Ontario, by pushing a wheelbarrow 74.07 metres. So what's the big deal? Well, the wheelbarrow was loaded with 3781.36 kilograms of bricks.

Frequent Flyers

During the summer months, brightly coloured orange, black and white monarch butterflies are always on the move, flitting from flower to flower to fuel up on nectar. But when the days start to get shorter and the nights a little cooler, they set out on an incredible 4000-kilometre journey all the way from southern Canada to central Mexico. Many of them don't make it, but about 300 million do. The spring migration north is a more leisurely affair. It takes three or four generations of monarchs to complete the trip back to Canada. How does each new butterfly know where to go when it emerges from its chrysalis? That is still a mystery.

What's That, Eh?

According to *The Canadian Oxford Dictionary*, keener is a Canadian term used to describe the type of student most teachers wished they had more of in their classes. Neat, eh?

... that, on average, the coldest day of the year in Canada is February 6? And the warmest? That's usually on or about July 17.

DID YOU KNOW...

How Bad Was It?

The Great Depression of the 1930s was a very difficult time for many Canadians. Hundreds of thousands were out of work, and hungry people were forced to line up at government- or charity-run soup kitchens for free meals. Farmers on the drought-stricken prairies went broke, and city families who couldn't pay the rent lost their homes. But even hard times can produce some pretty tricky folk sayings. One popular Canadian saying that referred to someone wearily trudging from place to place looking for a job said it all: "His shoes were so thin, he could step on a dime and tell whether it was heads or tails."

And if you were wondering just how flat the prairie landscape could be, some Manitobans might point out that it's so flat and bare that "a woodpecker would have to pack a box lunch."

Speaking of Canadian folk sayings, here's one that a grandmother could use when a visiting grandchild was behaving so unbelievably well that she wondered what was up. She'd look the little angel in the eye and say, "You're so sweet, you make my teeth ache."

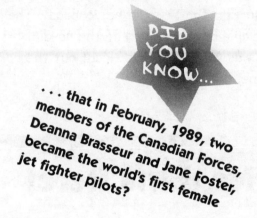

DID YOU KNOW...

... that in February, 1989, two members of the Canadian Forces, Deanna Brasseur and Jane Foster, became the world's first female jet fighter pilots?

Snowballs

April 7, 1977 ... Spring training had ended and the baseball season was underway. Over 44 500 eager fans crowded into Toronto's Exhibition Stadium for the very first home game of the Toronto Blue Jays. But by the end of the game it wasn't just the new Canadian team's uniforms that were blue. The *fans* were turning blue too. It snowed during the game and, with the wind chill factored in, it was -10°C in the outdoor stadium. Thank goodness the Jays pulled off a 9-5 win over the Chicago White Sox. At least the fans went home with warm hearts.

Hold Your Tongue, or Else . . .

. . . You'll lose it. At one time that was the warning given to residents of New France. The eighth time you were caught using profanity could be your last. The punishment for an eighth violation of the no-dirty-language order was very effective — cut out the offending tongue.

Get Me Outta Here!

One big problem early Canada had to cope with was fire. Entire settlements could be reduced to charred rubble by fires that started in dirty soot-filled chimneys, so regular chimney cleaning was often compulsory. However, people obviously didn't pay too much attention to the poor chimney sweeps who had to crawl down into the chimneys and clean them out. Why else would the *Quebec Gazette* have printed a notice to readers in September, 1772, reminding them to put out fires in the fireplaces *before* the sweeps started work?

No TV Watching Allowed

Thinking about bringing a portable TV along on your next car trip, or having one installed in your limo when you become a millionaire? Well, just in case you can't figure it out on your own, Ontario has a law that will help you decide where not to put it. You can't have a TV on the dashboard, and you can't have one turned on in the front seat. In other words, you can't drive and watch television at the same time. No kidding!

What's That, Eh?

Ski-doo isn't just a brand name anymore. The original name given by Armand Bombardier to his invention has now become a Canadian word in and of itself. Companies other than Bombardier must become a little frustrated when people call their products skidoos and talk about going skidooing.

Tree Tops

Of the ten biggest trees in North America, six are found in beautiful British Columbia, and they're all Western red cedars. Biggest doesn't mean tallest. It's a combination of height, trunk thickness and how wide the branching, leafy top (crown) spreads out.

The tallest tree in Canada is a Sitka spruce in B.C.'s Carmanah Pacific Provincial Park. This majestic spruce towers nearly 96 metres above the ground. Another B.C. giant, a Douglas fir in Strathcona Provincial Park, comes second at just under 83 metres.

What's That, Eh?

Don't expect visitors to know what you're talking about the first time you mention a loony (also loonie) or a toony (also toonie or twoonie). You may be too young to remember what life was like before these two coins replaced the one- and two-dollar bills, so you might not realize that these terms are just nicknames, and not official terms for the currency.

Great Lakes

The Great Lakes really are great. Superior, with a surface area of 82 414 square kilometres, is the largest freshwater lake in the world. What's more, Canada has nine of the ten largest freshwater lakes in North America. Starting with the largest, they are: Lake Superior (obviously), Lake Huron, Great Bear Lake, Great Slave Lake, Lake Erie, Lake Winnipeg, Lake Ontario, Lake Athabaska, and Reindeer Lake. Lake Michigan, in the U.S., comes in at third largest in North America, right after Lake Huron.

And in the middle of one of those great lakes lies the largest fresh-water island in the world — Manitoulin Island in Lake Huron. Manitoulin is big enough to have its own island in a lake. So, that island — Mindemoya — is an island in a lake on an island in a lake. Got that?

DID YOU KNOW...

. . . that most Christmas trees sold during the holiday season are 10 years old when they're cut down?

That's Some Log Cabin

Montebello, Quebec, west of Montreal, is home to Le Château Montebello. This impressive resort hotel has the distinction of being the biggest log building in the world. Erected in 1930 by the Canadian Pacific Railway (CPR), it was built out of 100 000 red cedar logs brought by train all the way from British Columbia. More than 3000 men, working mainly by hand, assembled the logs in just two months, a feat nearly as impressive as the building itself.

Société Historique Louis-Joseph, Montebello, Québec

It's A Bird . . . It's A Plane . . . It's A Star!

It may seem hard to believe, but far too many Canadians have never really seen the night sky. Because of all the light pollution in areas where most Canadians live, the night sky appears as a pale imitation of the real thing. Even on the clearest of nights the glow of big cities still outshines the spectacular beauty of the heavens.

But in the summer of 1999 Ontario became the first place in the world to announce plans for a dark-sky park. A 1900-hectare piece of province-owned land known as the Torrance Barrens has been set aside to be preserved as a light-free zone. Like provincial and national parks set aside to protect plant and animal life and the natural landscape, the area south of Lake Muskoka and west of Gravenhurst will protect the skyscape from light pollution. All together now: "Twinkle, twinkle, little star . . . "

Silence is Golden

It used to be illegal in Manitoba to sing while using "the facilities," if the outhouse was attached to an eating establishment or tavern where wine was served. Who knows what riotous melodies might have drifted through the walls into the dining room if that law hadn't been in place. As for what else might have drifted through the walls, that's another story . . .

Liar,
Liar

Elected members still have to watch what they say when they're debating in Parliament and provincial legislatures. None of them can call another member a liar — it's an example of "unparliamentary language." The forbidden word list for Members of Parliament also includes such choice phrases as "bag of wind," "evil genius" and "political sewer pipes." In the Ontario legislature, "vulture" is taboo, and "fat, wingless duck" is a no-no in Alberta.

Towering Above the Rest

When it was built in 1975, Toronto's amazing 555-metre-high CN Tower was the tallest free-standing structure in the world, now surpassed by the Burj Dubai. On a clear day, when you look out from the observation floor at the 447-metre level, you can see all the way across Lake Ontario to Niagara Falls.

George Kapeynes of Hamilton, Ontario, didn't show up at the Tower on October 27, 1985, to do some sightseeing, though. He was there to climb its 1760 stairs, and he did it in a record-breaking 8 minutes, 28 seconds.

What's That, Eh?

In a rugby scrum, packs of players huddle over a ball on the ground and try to gain control of it using only their feet. But Canadians came up with another, very effective use of the word. It's the name given to that wild scene you see on the news when a crowd of reporters surrounds a politician, hoping to get him or her to answer the questions they're shouting out. Caught in a scrum, a politician may very well feel like a battered rugby ball.

Christmas Crush

Robert Waller worked as a clerk at the Wal-Mart store in Fredericton, New Brunswick. On December 14, 1996, he was injured on the job. He was rushed to hospital with a concussion, several broken ribs, an injured back and leg, and cuts and bruises over much of his body. He was off work for six months recovering from those injuries.

Did the store roof or a huge stack of cast-iron pots come crashing down on Waller? No. What hit him was a crowd of frenzied Christmas shoppers. They trampled him underfoot when they spotted him opening a box of newly arrived Tickle Me Elmo dolls. The dolls were all the rage that year, and some people were willing to pay thousands of dollars to get one. Waller was just one of many unfortunate victims struck down by the Elmo virus. Bah, humbug.

Mega-Sizzlers

When the J. M. Schneider Company and M&M Meats in Kitchener, Ontario, got together on a sausage-making feat, they were unbeatable. In September, 1983, they stuffed a 14.17-kilometre-long sausage coil with nearly 7950 kilograms of ground pork and seasonings. In 1990, a team in England knocked them off the Guinness record podium with a 21-kilometre-long effort. But in 1997 the Kitchener team was back with a vengeance. Over two days in April, they ground out a 46-kilometre-long whopper.

··· that at the turn of the millennium, Canadians were drinking about 15 billion cups of coffee and about 7 billion cups of tea a year? But nearly 5 million Canucks probably switch to things like hot lemon juice and honey or chicken soup for a week or two each winter. Why? Because up to 5 million Canadians get the flu annually.

Not Very Ladylike, Eh?

On May 30, 1899, a Canadian woman named Pearl Hart pulled off the last stagecoach hold-up in the United States. After finishing her regular education, Hart had gone to a special finishing school for proper young ladies in her home town of Lindsay, Ontario. But then she ran away from home and ended up in Colorado, where she hung out with Martha Jane Canary — better known as Calamity Jane — a sharp-shooting star of Wild West shows, and the girlfriend of Wild Bill Hickok.

Bird on the Run

On November 6, 1997, a fugitive named Elisha was spotted on the Ottawa River trying to hide out among a flock of Canada geese. But she stood out like a pink flamingo in that crowd, and it wasn't long before some worried bird-watchers were hot on her trail.

Elisha was in fact a real flamingo that had escaped back in early September from a greenhouse on her wealthy owner's New England estate. After a month of outwitting her American pursuers, she went into hiding. Now she was back in plain view, but no one could catch her, and time was running out. With winter on the way, Elisha was in danger of starving or freezing to death. Finally, in mid-December, some volunteers managed to snag her in the river with a net. So, Ottawans said goodbye to Elisha and to any fantasies they might have had about living in the new Florida of the north.

Linked to the Past

It all started on March 11, 1965. That's the day Gary Duschl of Waterdown, near Hamilton, Ontario, first picked up a Wrigley's gum wrapper, tore it in half lengthwise, and after a few careful folds, slipped one part into the other to form the first two links of a gum wrapper chain. Kids have been making gum wrapper chains ever since Wrigley's first came out with JUICY FRUIT, Spearmint and DOUBLEMINT, so what Duschl did that day wasn't a big deal. But the fact that he's still adding to that chain decades later is.

By 2000 Duschl's chain was more than 8 kilometres long and weighed about 170 kilograms. Lying in bins in his basement, it looked like a long, thin yellow-and-green snake waiting to slither out onto the floor. Ripley's Entertainment offered to buy it for one of its Believe It or Not!® museums, but Duschl said no. He had only linked up about 650 000 wrappers by then, and he was aiming for a million.

By the mid-2000s Duschl folded his way well past the million-gum wrapper mark, and by March 2009, he had linked 1 370 166 wrappers together to make a chain 17 760 metres long.

GIVE US BACK OUR HEAD

Staff at Ripley's Believe It or Not!® Museum in Niagara Falls, Ontario, were left scratching their heads in February, 2000, as they tried to figure out why anyone would want to steal the museum's most famous item — a wizened, black-haired shrunken head. Even if the

thief knew that the head was worth more than $20 000, he or she would have a hard time selling it without attracting police attention. For the same reason, it would be really dumb to hang it on the wall at home. But who'd want something like that hiding in a box under the bed?

THE Gardens

It's been dubbed the "temple of hockey." It's also been called "Make-Believe Gardens" because of how loyal Toronto Maple Leaf fans remain even though their team hasn't won a Stanley Cup championship since 1967. Built in 1931, the Gardens quickly became the best known hockey arena in all of North America. It was home to the Leafs until they moved to the new Air Canada Centre in February, 1999.

But hockey isn't the Gardens' only claim to fame. British prime minister Winston Churchill gave a speech in the

Gardens over 70 years ago. Elvis Presley drove the girls wild at two back-to-back Gardens concerts in 1957, and the Beatles had fans fainting all over the place when they played there in 1964. And in 1966, Canadian boxer George Chuvalo went face to face with the heavyweight champion of the world, Muhammad Ali. That match made boxing history. Ali won the fight, but Chuvalo was the only opponent ever to last a full 15 rounds with the king of the ring.

And speaking of Elvis . . .

Elvis Presley went on to Ottawa following his Gardens appearance in April, 1957. There he gave two more performances that definitely left those in attendance all shook up. The next day, April 4, a local newspaper reported that eight young ladies had been expelled from Notre Dame Convent for disobeying a school ban against attending such an immoral event.

Elvis never got to give his next scheduled concert in Verdun, Quebec. That event was cancelled to prevent the corruption of local youth. Four months later, on August 31, Elvis returned to Canada to perform in front of a crowd of 25 000 at Empire Stadium in Vancouver. The show ended after just 45 minutes when rioting fans rushed onto the field.

Those three "Elvis sightings" put Canada on the trivia map as the only foreign country The King ever performed in.

DID YOU KNOW...

...that the Stanley Cup, awarded each year to the champions of the National Hockey League, is one of the very few major professional sports trophies that players can take home and show off to their friends? And did you know that Kenora, Ontario, is the smallest community ever to give the cup a home for a year? It happened when the Kenora Thistles won the championship in 1907.

Dinner's Ready!

Cooks in Elgin, Manitoba, had an easy time of it on April 22, 1932. The main course landed in town, cooked and ready to serve, when lightning bolts struck a flock of wild geese flying overhead. The zapped birds fell to the ground crisp and sizzling, so there was no point in letting them go to waste.

All Bugged Up

Early computers were giants when compared to today's desktops and laptops, but they weren't nearly as "smart" as the newer mini-models. In fact, one computer was an absolute dunce. In 1965 the Ministry of Education in Quebec put one of the new-fangled machines to work marking province-wide Grade 11 exams. It failed miserably, making mistakes correcting every single one of the 7000 tests. Give that computer an F!

Winnie the Canuck

The English claim him as their own. He's Christopher Robin's lovable bear buddy, Winnie-the-Pooh. Created by an English writer, A. A. Milne, the character was based on a small black bear named Winnie who was a hugely popular resident of the London Zoo. But residents of White River, Ontario, northwest of Sault Ste. Marie, know better. They know that the original Winnie is Canadian through and through.

In 1913, a trapper found an orphaned black bear cub and took her to White River where she could be fed and cared for. A year later a Canadian veterinarian, Harry Colebourn, spotted the bear when the train taking him to Toronto to join other World War I soldiers stopped in White River. Colebourn bought the bear, named her Winnie after his home town, Winnipeg, and took her with him to England as the mascot of his army regiment, the 2nd Canadian Infantry Brigade. Winnie was sent to the London Zoo when the regiment left to fight in France. Milne and his son, Christopher Robin, were two of the many visitors who loved to go to the zoo to watch Winnie.

And that's how a Canadian bear got a starring role in a British children's classic, and why both White River and Winnipeg have statues honouring the world-famous, honey-loving resident of Pooh Corner.

Them's Fighting Words

Thirty-one-year-old David Boys of Montreal made history in London, England, on November 5, 1995, when he became the first Canadian ever to win the World Scrabble Championship. Boys, who had been playing for only 10 years, beat out 64 competitors from 31 countries to win $15 000 and a gold-plated Scrabble set. Boys came up with two terrific "vowel dumps" during the final match — iota and aioli. (What do they mean? Get out the dictionary. And while you're at it, see if you can find his last word of the game — lud.)

Two years after Boys' victory, Canada held its first national Scrabble championship from October 18–20 in Toronto. After a gruelling 18-game marathon, 21-year-old Adam Logan of Ottawa emerged victorious. It was Logan's second major win that year. Four months earlier, he had won $25 000 when he came first at the North American Scrabble Championship held in Dallas, Texas. A math student working on his Ph.D. at Harvard University, Logan entered his first Scrabble contest when he was only 9. Peter Morris, the man Logan beat in the final game of the Canadian championship, was no Scrabble pushover, either. A former Canadian who moved to the United States, he was listed in the *Guinness Book of World Records* as the only person to win both the North American and World Championships.

Hammy Hunters

The most popular Canadian children's pet at the turn of the new millennium was the hamster, a furry little rodent made even more popular because so many youngsters want to have their own "Hammy." Hammy was the star of the Canadian TV program, *Once Upon a Hamster*. The show had been such a hit with viewers in 22 countries that hamster breeders were having trouble supplying pet shops with the top-selling breeds.

All Shook Up in Cottage Country

The T-shirt reads:
I SPENT THE WEEKEND WITH ELVIS IN COLLINGWOOD.
But maybe it should actually read: I spent the weekend with *lots* of Elvises, because hundreds of them, complete with sequin-covered jumpsuits and slicked-back hair, turn up in Collingwood, Ontario, each summer for the annual Canadian Elvis Tribute and Convention. The first Collingwood Elvisfest was held July 28-30, 1995. Ever since that first success, thousands of visitors have crowded into Collingwood for a week or so to step on each other's blue suede shoes, and they can't help falling in love with the place. Little sisters, hard-headed women and Bossa Nova babies gather to cheer on their big hunks of love who are hoping to win prizes for the best sideburns, the best jumpsuit, and the best on-stage imitation. Judges know it may be now or never for some of the older E.P. wannabes, so they hand out a prize for the oldest Elvis, too.

Big Nickel

On a clear day, you can't miss it. It's the Big Nickel — Sudbury, Ontario's, best-known landmark — and it really is big. It's 9 metres across and 61 centimetres thick, making it the largest coin in the world. This giant replica of a 1951 five-cent piece marks the entrance to the Big Nickel Mine, the only hardrock mine in Ontario that is open to visitors. The mine gives tourists a glimpse into the life of a hardrock miner, and is also home to the only underground mailbox in Canada.

One item that uses up at least 25 000 tonnes of nickel a year is the stainless steel sink found in kitchens around the world. It was the brainchild of Harry Galley, who was born in Arundel, Quebec. Galley was an Inco sales executive. In the 1930s, he got the idea to replace

Paul Heersink

enamel-coated cast-iron sinks with stainless steel ones that wouldn't chip and were very easy to clean. But it wasn't until the 1940s that Inco agreed to pay for developing his idea in a serious way. Galley finally patented his sink design in 1948, and the rest is kitchen history.

Sanitation for the Nation

That was the motto of G. H. Wood and Co. Ltd., a company founded by George Hutchence Wood of Toronto, Ontario. Worried about the way diseases could spread when people shared the same drinking cup, especially in public places, he started a company to make paper-shaped cones. *Voilà* – the first disposable paper cup!

From 1950 to 1975, Wood's company display at the Canadian National Exhibition (CNE) wowed visitors to the annual fair. Each year Wood filled his display with a million dollars in bills, silver dollars and gold coins, to show everyone how much money businesses lost every day when people stayed home sick from illnesses caused by unhealthy, dirty workplaces. He prided himself in knowing that his company's sanitary products were in more public washrooms than any other firm's.

DID YOU KNOW...

· · · that Canada has two official sports? Lacrosse was most popular with Canadians until the 1900s and was the first organized sport in North America. Then hockey started to win over Canadian fans, and the debate was on as to which sport should have official status. Finally, in May, 1994, a bill giving both sports that honour became law.

In the Eye of the Beholder

Year after year, a giant steel magnet draws tourists to one of New Brunswick's most popular attractions, Magnetic Hill near Moncton. After driving up the famous hill, people put their cars in neutral, and let them roll back down the hill. But as they roll down, their eyes tell them that they're actually rolling up the hill. It's all an optical illusion caused by the surrounding landscape — but knowing that doesn't spoil the fun. Visiting Magnetic Hill is just one of those things you have to do when you're on holiday.

Not Clever

One day in January, 1995, a would-be thief walked into a drugstore in Vernon, British Columbia, and told a clerk he was coming back in half an hour to rob the place. Sure enough, 30 minutes later he returned with a sidekick to help him carry out his big caper. But the two men barely made it in the door, let alone out of it with the loot. They walked right into the waiting arms of RCMP officers.

Double Duty

In 1858, John Butt was looking for work. He decided to go into business for himself in Victoria, British Columbia, a former fort that was quickly becoming a bustling new town. Butt offered his services to the town as a street cleaner, and worked out a fee to clean two streets — Governor Street and Yates Street — when they got really dirty. Then Butt set to work. First, he would scrape up and cart away the garbage, sludge and horse droppings from Governor Street. Then he'd drive to nearby Yates Street and, when no one was looking, he'd spread the filthy load there. After getting paid for cleaning Governor, he'd move along to Yates and get paid for cleaning *it*. And where did he put the filth from Yates? Right back on Governor! Victoria officials finally caught on to Butt's scam, but not before he had pocketed some decent change at the colony's expense.

Toilet Tales

Ever since 1977, Labour Day Weekend celebrations in Dawson City, Yukon, have included two special events — the Great International Outhouse Race and the Bathroom Wall Limerick Contest. The outhouse race is a 3-kilometre effort for four people in each five-member team that enters. They're the ones who actually carry their outhouse that far. The fifth member of the team has the privilege of sitting on the "throne" for the race through town. In the evening, teams gather at a local tavern to recite five-line limericks about their outhouse. Most of the verses are pretty . . . well . . . crappy.

Miraculous Recovery

No one is absolutely certain how little Karlee Kosolofski managed to slip out of her house in the wee hours of the morning on February 23, 1994. But the two-year-old from Regina, Saskatchewan, did exactly that on a bitterly cold night when temperatures plunged to -22°C. Karlee was outside in only her pyjamas for nearly six hours before she was found. By then her body temperature was just 14.2°C, way below the normal body temperature of about 37°C.

Karlee's parents thought she must be dead. Even doctors figured it was most unlikely that she could be revived. But they didn't give up hope. Over several hours they slowly and carefully warmed her little body and, amazingly, Karlee began to show signs of life.

Karlee did lose part of her left leg to frostbite, but her recovery was complete in every other way, and the "miracle child" became the first person in the world ever to survive such a low recorded body temperature.

Honouring a Japanese Tradition

Y ou might not expect a Canadian stamp to have a picture of a sumo wrestler on it, but in June, 1998, Canada Post issued two such stamps. They celebrated a very special event that took place in Vancouver on June 6-7 that year. For only the ninth time in its 1500-year history, sumo wrestling held an official tournament, or *basho*, outside Japan. Vancouver's tournament was the first *basho* ever held in Canada.

© Canada Post Corporation, 1998. Reproduced by permission.

Rulers of the Pumpkin Patch

Months of tender loving care finally paid off for pumpkin growers John and Chris Lyons on October 2, 1994. That day they presented their big baby for the official weigh-in at the annual Pumpkinfest held in Port Elgin, Ontario, and learned that it had set a new world record. It weighed in at an amazing 408 kilograms!

In 1999 two Canadians, Todd Kline and Al Eaton, stood second and third in a competition to grow the biggest Atlantic Giant Pumpkin, a breed favoured by growers serious about producing really, really big pumpkins. Kline's Giant weighed 471.13 kilograms and Eaton's was a 456.86-kilogram wonder. Now there's a jack-o'-lantern!

What's That, Eh?

If your cat chewed up part of your science fair project, and your little brother decorated the display board with his new markers, you might say that you're fed up with the whole shebang. No one's sure of the origin of shebang, but it popped up in Canada sometime in the nineteenth century, and it's still hanging around. "The whole shebang" means the whole situation, the whole lot or the whole thing.

DID YOU KNOW...

... that you can visit one of the best bonsai collections in the world right here in Canada? The marvellous miniature trees are growing in Montreal's Jardin Botanique.

Altona, Front and Centre

Want to find the geographic centre of North America? Then look no further than Altona, Manitoba, south of Winnipeg near the American border. But that's not the only reason to check out Altona. It's also known as the sunflower capital of Canada and, some say, maybe even of the world. To celebrate the famous local crop, Altona greets visitors with a pretty impressive roadside attraction — the world's largest painting propped up on the world's largest easel. It's 7.3 metres wide and 9.8 metres high, and it's mounted on a 24.4-metre-tall easel. And the picture on the easel? You guessed it — a still-life study of sunflowers!

A Generous Canadian

Canada's best known poem around the world is "In Flanders Fields." The poem was written by a Canadian army doctor, Lt.-Col. John McCrae, to remind people of the soldiers who gave their lives fighting in World War I. The poem, written in 1915, three years before McCrae died while serving in France, has touched the hearts of millions.

McCrae's war medals had been in the hands of a private collector for years, but were put up for sale in 1977. The trouble was, neither a museum dedicated to McCrae's memory nor the National War Museum in Ottawa could come up with the money — expected to top $20 000 — to buy them. Enter Toronto businessman Arthur Lee, who had come to Canada from China when he was 12.

People were concerned that the McCrae medals might be bought by someone who didn't live in Canada, and that this small but significant part of Canadian history would be lost to the country forever. Arthur Lee didn't know about their fears when he showed up at the auction, but about half an hour before the bidding began, he happened to read the poem and information about McCrae in a small brochure. The poem so moved Lee that, when the bidding on the medals soared to an amazing $300 000, he bid $400 000! The medals were his . . . but not for long. The next week, Lee donated them to what he felt was their rightful home — the McCrae Museum in Guelph, Ontario, John McCrae's home town.

What a Kid!

When 13-year-old Canadian diver Alexandre Despatie made his gold-medal platform dive at the 1998 Commonwealth Games in Kuala Lumpur, Malaysia, he entered the record books for more than his winning dive. He also became the world's youngest winner of an international diving competition.

Chinook – Not Just a Warm Wind

In August, 1994, a new computer program called Chinook became the new world checkers champion. The apparently unbeatable champ was Canadian, and it was fast as well as good. Its creator, University of Alberta professor Jonathan Schaeffer, had figured out a way to compress the incredible amount of information Chinook had to keep in its "head" to play a winning game. In 1997 Chinook retired from competition to give humans a crack at the championship again.

DID YOU KNOW...

... that Canada's most famous resident has his own postal code? To reach Mr. S. Claus at the North Pole, simply address your cards and letters to him at the Pole and add his code, H0H 0H0.

How long does it take him to reach all the good boys and girls each December? Supposedly, to finish his marathon sleigh ride in just 24 hours, he would have to travel at 112 kilometres per second, stopping for just 1/20 000th of a second at each chimney. Go, Santa!

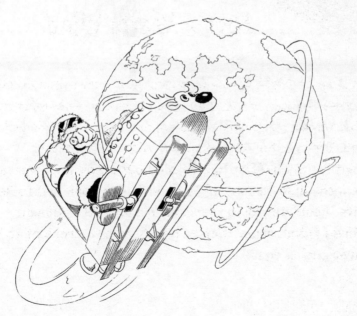

... that the paper used to make Canadian money, manufactured at a mill in Beauharnois, Quebec, is one-quarter wood pulp and three-quarters cotton? The cotton, which gives the bills strength, comes from bluejeans factories in Montreal. They ship all the bits and trimmings that are left over to the papermaking plant in Beauharnois.

Sharing the Candlelight

Clayton Simko of Windsor was born on February 15, 1994. His sister was delighted. She was born on February 15, so baby Clayton was a great birthday present. Mom was pretty excited about the arrival date too, because February 15 was *her* birthday as well. And believe it or not, Clayton shared his birthday with his great-grandmother too!

They Did It First

Edward "Ned" Hanlan (1855–1908), a rower from Toronto, was Canada's first world champion athlete. Hanlan become the Canadian champion single sculler — that's a rower in a one-person lightweight boat — in 1877, and won the American championship in 1878. Then he headed off to England to take on the world champion, Australian E. A. Trickett, in 1879. Hanlan didn't just win. He beat Trickett to the finish line by an amazing

11 lengths, and took home Canada's first world championship trophy.

In September, 1904, at the Olympic Games held in St. Louis, Missouri, Montrealer Étienne Desmarteau became the first Canadian to win Olympic gold for Canada. He came first in the 56-pound (25.45-kilogram) hammer throw event.

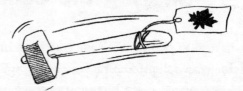

On September 20, 1954, Toronto long-distance swimmer Marilyn Bell became the first person ever to swim across Lake Ontario. She was just 16 at the time. A year later, she became the youngest person ever to swim across the English Channel.

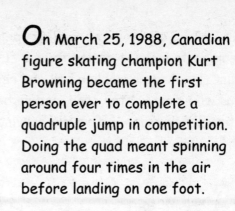

On March 25, 1988, Canadian figure skating champion Kurt Browning became the first person ever to complete a quadruple jump in competition. Doing the quad meant spinning around four times in the air before landing on one foot.

In the 1950s, Montreal Canadiens star Jacques Plante became the first goaltender to make a habit of skating around to the back of his net to stop the puck and pass it to one of his teammates. And,

fed up with getting hit in the face with a puck, he was also the first goalie to start wearing a mask.

On September 23, 1992, Manon Rhéaume of Lac Beauport, Quebec, put on her mask and goalie pads and played one period of an NHL exhibition game for the Tampa Bay Lightning, making her the first woman ever to play professional hockey.

In 1909, Toronto bowling alley operator Tom Ryan decided to make it easier for his customers to play the game. He made a smaller ball and replaced the ten heavy pins with five lighter ones, and so became the father of a brand new game — five-pin bowling.

What's That, Eh?

To Canadians and Americans alike, a beater isn't only what you use to whip up scrambled eggs or cake batter. It's also an old car that's in really rough shape but still manages to sputter and chug around town. But faced with cold winters, Canadians stuck with a beaten up old clunker aren't as badly off if it's "a beater with a heater." The expression speaks for itself.

Phony as a Three-Dollar Bill?

Canadians used to have three-dollar bills, but they were officially done away with in 1871. Still, St. Stephen's Bank in New Brunswick kept on issuing them for another 15 years. And 25-cent bills weren't phony in Canada from 1870 to 1935. They were issued in 1870, 1900 and 1923, at times when there weren't enough quarters to go around. Because they weren't much bigger than a large Band-Aid, people called them "shinplasters." The Bank of Canada phased them out in 1935.

A Big Bonanza

You may have heard that Canada is home to the world's biggest *pysanka*, a brightly decorated Ukrainian Easter egg. Located in Vegreville, Alberta, it's 9.45 metres tall, 7.8 metres long and 5.5 metres wide.

And you've most likely heard of the Wawa Goose in Wawa, Ontario. This 2-tonne wrought-iron sculpture stands 9 metres tall, is 7 metres long, and is 6 metres wide from wingtip to wingtip.

But would you believe a 10.7-metre-long, 50-tonne lobster? Well, believe it. It's in Shediac, New Brunswick.

Naturally, Turtleford, Saskatchewan, has Big Ernie, an 8.5-metre-long turtle, and it seems only fitting that Moonbeam, Ontario, would greet its visitors with a 5.5-metre-wide flying saucer. But what do folks think when they visit Komarno, Manitoba, for the first time and encounter a giant mosquito with a 4.6-metre wingspan?

A Long Shot

Back in 1992, 22-year-old Jason Zuback walloped a golf ball all the way from the fourth hole tee to the green at the Land-O-Lakes Golf and Country Club in his home town of Coaldale, Alberta. Zuback's ball travelled an amazing 467.26 metres, making him the only player ever to have hit a golf ball that far.

Hitting farther than anyone else in the world is what Zuback does best. In 1996 and 1997 he won the North American Long Drive Championship, and in 1998 and 1999, he was the World Long Drive Champion. A ball hit by Zuback was measured going 336 kilometres per hour. His goal is to hit golf balls as far as is humanly possible.

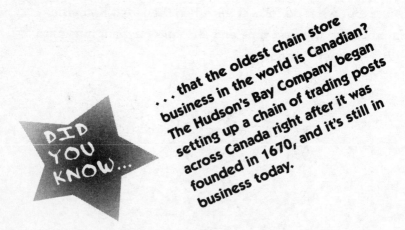

DID YOU KNOW...

. . . that the oldest chain store business in the world is Canadian? The Hudson's Bay Company began setting up a chain of trading posts across Canada right after it was founded in 1670, and it's still in business today.

King
of the Dance Floor

From June 28 to July 3, 1983, Alain Dumas danced the days and nights away at a place called the Disco Shop in Granby, Quebec. Nine young women took turns waltzing and two-stepping with him during the non-stop display of his dancing skills. After 120 hours and 30 minutes, Dumas took a bow. He had just established a new individual world record for non-stop ballroom dancing.

DID YOU KNOW...

...that teachers receive more valentines than any other group?

DID YOU KNOW...

. . . that the Anna depicted in the films *The King and I* and *Anna and the King* lived in Canada for nearly forty years? The real Anna was Anna Leonowens, a widowed mother who supported her own two children by teaching the King of Siam's children to speak English. She came to Halifax in 1887, and moved to Montreal 12 years later. She died in Montreal in 1915.

DID YOU KNOW...

. . . that the word CYBERSPACE is the product of the creative Canadian mind of sci-fi writer William Gibson?

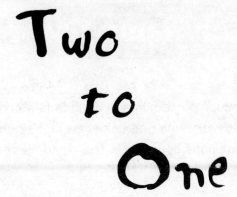

Two to One

A football goal post used to look like a giant letter H. Now it looks like a squared off letter Y or a slingshot, thanks to ex-Montreal Alouette coach Jim Trimble and former St. Mary's University coach Bob Hayes. In the mid-sixties, Trimble told Hayes he thought a single-post goal post would work better. It could be set back from the touchdown line, so players wouldn't crash into it as they often did when the two-pole posts were planted *on* the line.

Hayes liked the idea, made a couple out of scrap metal, and installed them on the St. Mary's field in Halifax. Around the same time, Trimble had an engineer named Cedric Marsh help him design and make a pair of the posts that he gave to the Alouettes to use in 1966. But it wasn't until the new design showed up at the next Orange Bowl game in Miami that pro football movers and shakers realized what an improvement it was. In 1967 the slingshot goal posts scored a touchdown when the National Football League decided they were the only way to go.

The Name Game

The most common place name in Canada is Mount Pleasant, with Centreville and Lakeview right behind in second. Pleasant pops up again in the third most common name, Pleasant Valley.

When it comes to geographic features such as lakes, islands, ponds and mountains, Long Lake is a clear winner in the name game, especially if you add it in with the third most common feature name, Lac Long. Mud Lake is tucked in between in second place.

Another clear winner emerges in the longest place name category. It's Cape St. George-Petit Jardin-Grand Jardin-De Grau-Marches Point-Loretto, a community in Newfoundland. Yikes!

DID YOU KNOW...

...that every day Canadians devour about 60 million slices of bread? Find that hard to believe? Think sandwiches.

DID YOU KNOW...

... that at least one meteorite of 100 grams or larger thuds into Canadian soil every day? But fewer than five dozen have ever been found because no one is around to hear or see them fall.

Apparently, a golf course, with its wide open spaces, is one of the best places to look for them. It would be easier to spot one there than in the woods or in a farmer's field.

DID YOU KNOW...

... that there's a chocolate scholarship out there just waiting for the right student? In 1998, Michael Comrie of Toronto was that student. The would-be chef won the Terry Miller Chocolate Scholarship from the New England Culinary Institute for his chocolate creation. And the name of the creation that wowed the judges? Rippled Chocolate Macadamia Nut Mini Bundt Cake with Ebony and Ivory Chocolate Sauce! Mmmmmmmm!

Lining Up to Sign Up

Back in 1942, Carl Lindley of Danville, Illinois, was a long way from home. He was part of a construction team building the Alaska Highway in the Yukon. In a homesick moment, he planted a signpost pointing the way back to Danville. His seedling sign grew into a forest as other visitors to the area followed his example. By 2009 the World-Famous Signpost Forest of Watson Lake, Yukon, was home to more than 64 000 signs pointing to places all over the globe.

DID YOU KNOW...

. . . that it's illegal to spit on city roads in Kanata, Ontario? The city passed the bylaw in 1999, supposedly to prevent damage to, or hazardous conditions on, the roads. No doubt about it, spitting is gross. But damaging or hazardous? Hmmmmm . . .

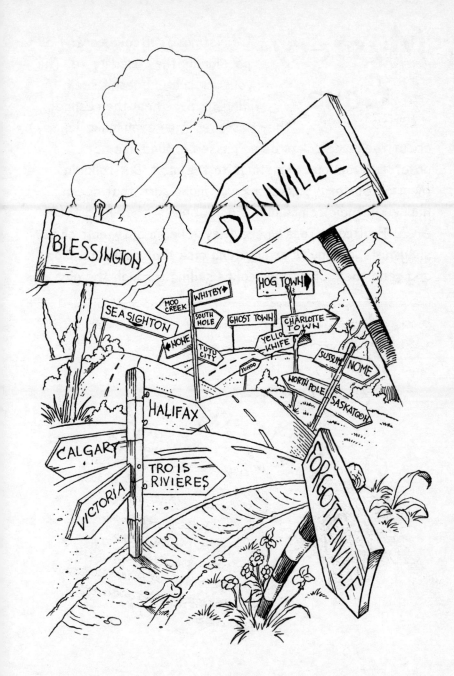

Mystery Cake

Christmas fruitcakes aren't as popular as they used to be. The younger crowd doesn't seem willing to give them the respect they deserve. They even make jokes about the same cakes being passed around like hot potatoes from one Christmas to the next. But folks in Manitou Springs, Saskatchewan, make sure that doesn't happen in their community. Each January they hold their Great Fruitcake Toss where they take up bats, golf clubs, slingshots, catapults or anything else that packs a wallop, and send their Christmas cakes sailing through the air.